All About Geometry

Written by Joyce Markovics

rourkeeducationalmedia.com

www.rourkeeducationalmedia.com

PHOTO CREDITS: Cover © Gerald Bernard; Title Page © Poznyakov; Page 3 © Paulmichaelhughes; Page 4 © Mcininch; Page 5 © Monkeybusinessimages; Page 6 © Wojpra; Page 11 © PhotoBeaM; Page 12 © aldomurillo; Page 17 © Murali Nath ; Page 18 © Blueperfume

Edited by Jill Sherman

Cover design by Tara Raymo

Interior design by Jen Thomas

Library of Congress PCN Data

All About Geometry / Joyce Markovics
(Little World Math)
ISBN 978-1-62169-888-3 (hard cover)
ISBN 978-1-62169-783-1 (soft cover)
ISBN 978-1-62169-987-3 (e-Book)
Library of Congress Control Number: 2013936805

Also Available as:

Rourke Educational Media
Printed in the United States of America,
North Mankato, Minnesota

Rourke
Educational Media

rourkeeducationalmedia.com
customerservice@rourkeeducationalmedia.com • PO Box 643328 Vero Beach, Florida 32964

What is geometry?
It is all about shapes and lines.

Let's learn about geometry by exploring shapes!

There are two types of shapes.
Some shapes are flat, and others are solid.

Flat shapes can be drawn on a flat surface called a plane.

Do you know these flat shapes?

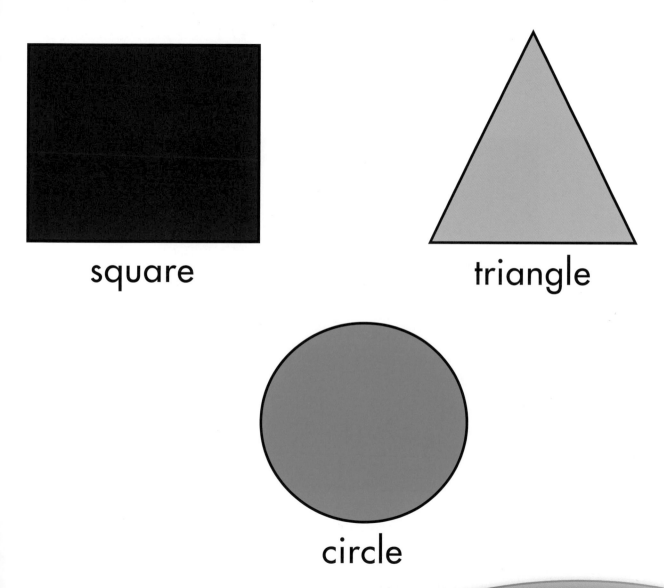

square

triangle

circle

Look at the red square.
How many sides does it have?

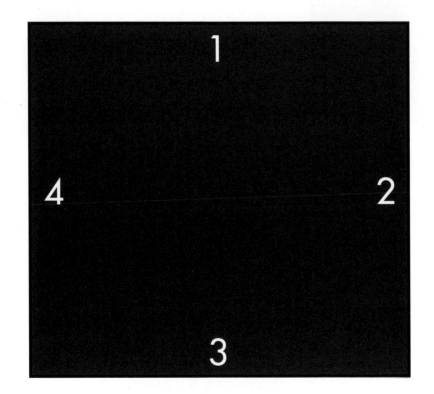

How many corners, or angles, does it have?

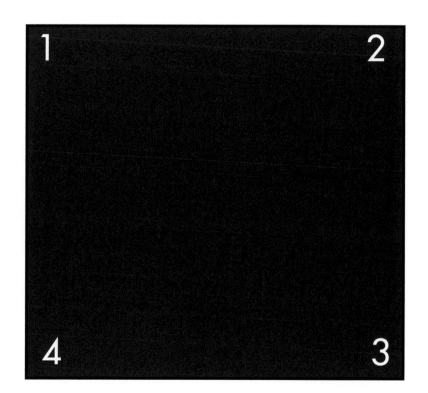

Any flat shape with four sides and four corners is called a quadrilateral.

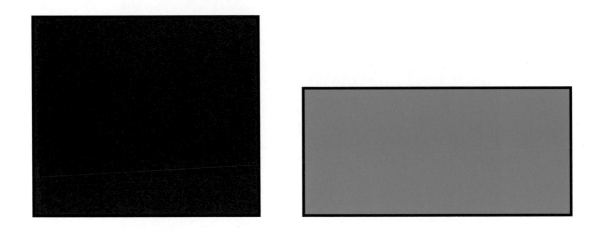

Try drawing your own quadrilateral!

Solid shapes have a greater number of sides and corners than flat shapes.

Can you name these solid shapes?

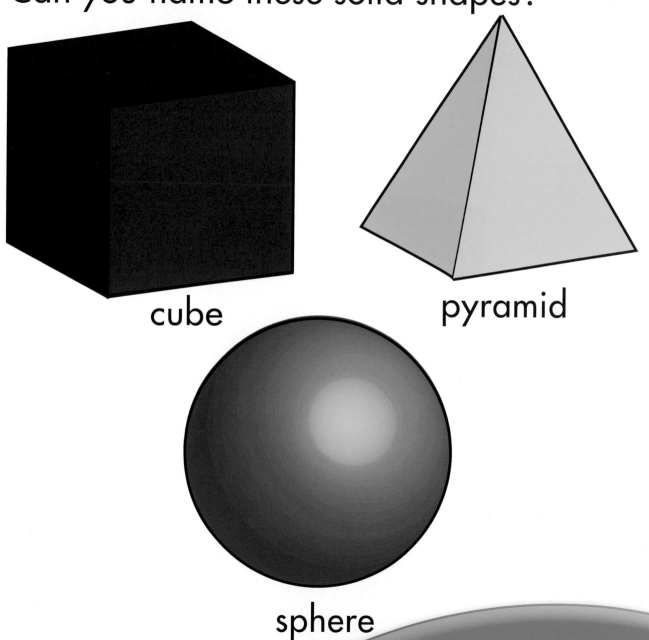

cube

pyramid

sphere

Look closely at the cube.
How many sides does it have?

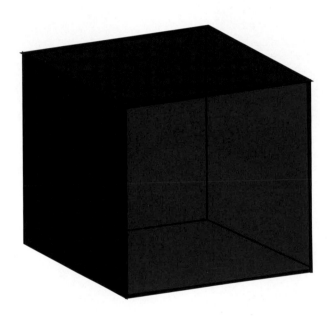

Does it have more or less sides and corners than a square? More! The cube has six sides and eight corners.

Any solid shape that has flat sides is called a polyhedra.

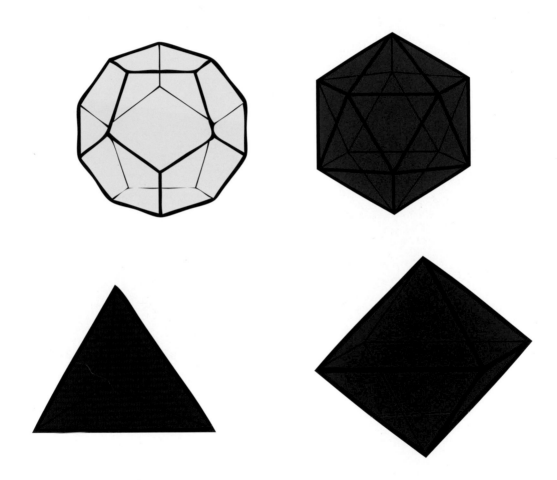

Think back to the cube. Is it a polyhedra?

Let's compare more shapes. Which one is flat?

Which one is solid? Here's a hint. The solid shape has more sides and corners.

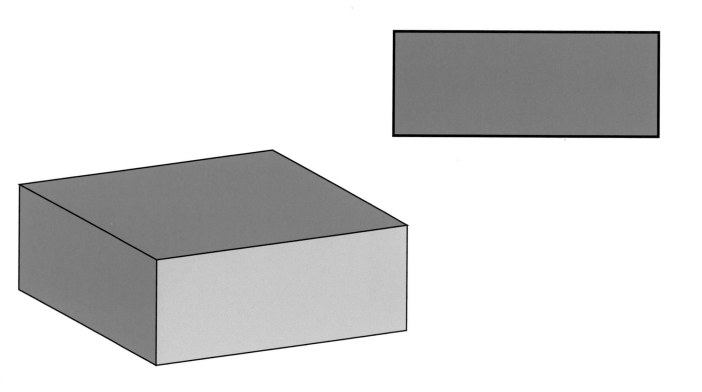

Look at all the shapes together. Which two shapes can you join together to make a rectangle?

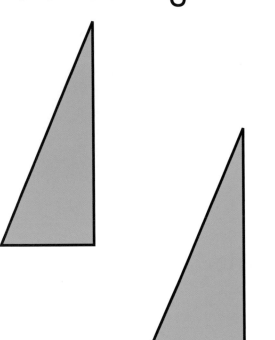

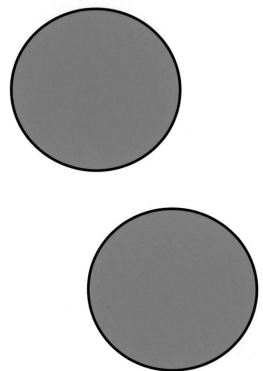

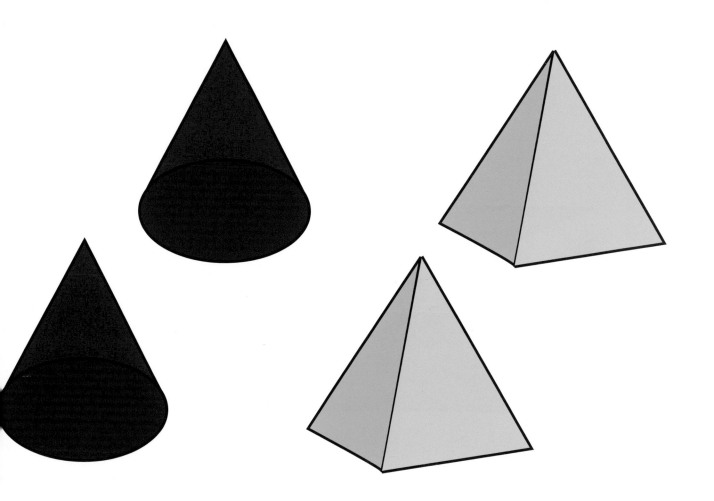

Will you need flat shapes or solid shapes?

Flat shapes! Which two shapes will form a rectangle?

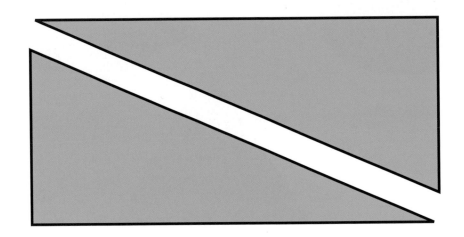

You got it! Two flat triangles form a rectangle.

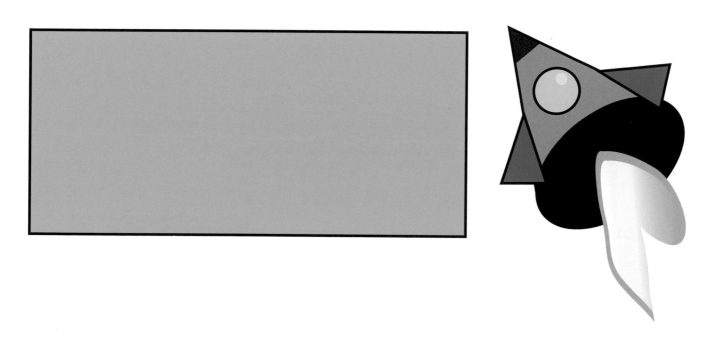

Geometry is a blast!

Index

Websites

www.abcya.com/shapes_geometry_game.htm
www.mathsisfun.com/geometry/index.html
pbskids.org/cyberchase/math-games/tanagram-game

About the Author

Joyce Markovics is a writer and editor. She shares her home in New York City with her husband, Adam, and a menagerie of pets that includes a spirited house rabbit named Pearl and a crooning frog. She has written over 20 books and enjoys thinking and writing about abstract concepts for young readers.

Meet The Author!
www.meetREMauthors.com

24